How I Learned Kindness from a Unicorn
My Unicorn Books - Volume 6
Written by Steve Herman

ISBN: 978-1-950280-29-2 (paperback)
ISBN: 978-1-950280-30-8 (hardcover)

www.MyUnicornBooks.com

First Edition: January 2020
10 9 8 7 6 5 4 3 2 1

Well, hello! I'm Allie McNally, and this is Dazzle D.
Dazzle is a unicorn, as I'm sure that you can see.

The D stands for "Delight," for she always seems to bring
Much happiness into my life and that's a wondrous thing.

But there is something else, as well, that Dazzle D can do –
She teaches me life lessons – Then I teach them all to you.

I'm young, so I have much to learn, and she's taught me a lot.
Listen as I tell you all about a lesson that she taught.

Later on that day, Tim dropped a crayon on the floor.
I stepped on it, so his crayon was no more...

Tim said, "Say you're sorry!" but I said, "Sorry? Why? It seems that we are even now." But Tim did not care for my reply.

We argued back and forth a bit. It wasn't very long
Before our teacher got involved and told me I was wrong.

I went home feeling kind of sad, but then my brother, Ben
Needed help with his math homework, as usual, once *again*!

I truly tried to help him learn! Honestly, I did!
But he wouldn't pay attention; he kept acting like a kid.

Since Ben would not behave himself, I tattled to our mother,
Who told me I should try to be much *kinder* to my brother.

I then gazed out my window, and I saw a rainbow's end –
Guess who was sliding down – It was Dazzle D, my friend!

I can always count on Dazzle D to be there by my side!
I opened wide the window and invited her inside.

DAZZLE D, PLEASE COME IN!

"Allie, girl," said Dazzle D, "I'm here to help you out;
I see you are confused and sad – What's this all about?"

So I told Dazzle D about the awful day I'd had,
How Tim and Ben had acted and why that made me feel bad.

"Everybody's telling me I really need to learn
That although sometimes other folks are not kind in return,
I should be kind to them. Does that sound fair to you?
Please advise me, Dazzle D. Tell me what to do!"

"I think I see the problem; you just need a small reminder
That life is so much sweeter when we practice being *kinder*."

"You *can't* control how others act, but, Allie, just decide
That you *CAN* control how you respond," Dazzle D replied.

"I know you were annoyed whenever Tim ate all your fries,
And he didn't say, 'I'm sorry,' but here's what I advise..."

"When you saw Tim had dropped his crayon,
the kinder thing to do...
Would have been to pick it up like you'd want done for *you*."

"And when you help your brother Ben
get his homework done,
Speak kind words of **encouragement**
to make the learning fun."

"And when he's being difficult, Allie, just recall,
That you were also much like Ben back when you were small."

"You see, it matters not one bit what others choose to do -
Make up your mind, no matter what,
that **kindness starts with *you*!**"

"I suggest you try it out; I'm pretty sure you'll find
That others will be kind in return whenever you are kind."

"And when someone needs a helping hand, ask what you can do."

"Be humble and apologize when you have made mistakes;
Be at peace with everyone, no matter what it takes."

So I started being kind like Dazzle said to do,
Before I even knew it, Tim was kinder, too.

And Ben is doing better since I've started being nice,
Because I chose to follow Dazzle's excellent advice.

I'll tell you something else I've found
that's really pretty cool —
Since I have been much kinder,
I have made new friends at school.

Kindness makes the world a better place!
It all begins with *you*.
When you are kind to others,
you're spreading kindness, too!"

READ MORE ABOUT ALLIE AND DAZZLE!

VISIT WWW.MYUNICORNBOOKS.COM

OTHER BOOKS BY STEVE HERMAN
MY DRAGON BOOKS SERIES

Made in the USA
Monee, IL
05 August 2023

40472923R00026

WWW.MYUNICORNBOOKS.COM

ISBN 9781950280292

9 781950 280292

90000

The Posh
Pescatarian

Stephanie Harris-Uyidi
My Favorite Sustainable Seafood Recipes